INTEGRATING
Our Community
with Reading Instruction

6 Complete Social Studies Units

Written by
Trisha Callella

Editor: LaDawn Walter
Illustrator: Jenny Campbell
Cover Illustrator: Rick Grayson
Designer/Production: Moonhee Pak/Terri Lamadrid
Cover Designer: Moonhee Pak
Art Director: Tom Cochrane
Project Director: Carolea Williams

Table of Contents

Introduction

For many children, reading comprehension diminishes when they read nonfiction text. Children often have difficulty understanding social studies vocabulary, making inferences, and grasping social studies concepts. With so much curriculum to cover each day, social studies content is sometimes put on the back burner when it comes to academic priorities. *Integrating Our Community with Reading Instruction* provides the perfect integration of social studies content with specific reading instruction to help children improve their comprehension of nonfiction text and maximize every minute of your teaching day.

This resource includes six units that relate to the theme of community. The units are based on the most common social studies topics taught in grades 1–2 in accordance with the national social studies standards:

Community Helpers	**Supply and Demand**
Good Citizens	**Kids in Business**
Responsible Spending	**Reading a Map**

Each unit includes powerful prereading strategies, such as predicting what the story will be about, accessing prior knowledge, and brainstorming about vocabulary that may be included in the reading selection. Following the prereading exercises is a nonfiction reading selection written on a grade 1–2 reading level. Each reading selection is followed by essential postreading activities such as comprehension questions on multiple taxonomy levels, skill reviews, and a critical thinking exercise. Each unit also includes a hands-on experience that connects each social studies topic to children's lives. The descriptions on pages 5–8 include the objectives and implementation strategies for each unit component.

Before, during, and after reading the story, children are exposed to the same reading strategies you typically reinforce during your language arts instruction block and guided reading. This powerful duo gives you the opportunity to teach both reading and social studies simultaneously. Using the activities in this resource, children will continue *learning to read* while *reading to learn*. They will become more successful readers while gaining new social studies knowledge and experiences.

Prereading Strategies

- ✓ Catch a Clue
- ✓ Concept Map
- ✓ Word Warm-Up

Nonfiction Text

Postreading Applications

- ✓ Comprehension Questions
- ✓ Sharpen Your Skills
- ✓ Get Logical

Hands-on Social Studies

Connections to Standards

This chart shows the concepts that are covered in each unit based on the national social studies standards.

	Community Helpers	Good Citizens	Responsible Spending	Supply and Demand	Kids in Business	Reading a Map
Describe personal connections to place—especially places associated with immediate surroundings.	●	●	●	●	●	●
Identify and describe ways family, groups, and community influence daily life and personal choices.	●	●	●	●	●	
Examine what it means to be a good citizen in the classroom, school, home, and community.		●	●			
Examine rights and responsibilities.		●				
Give examples that show how scarcity and choice direct our economic decisions.			●	●	●	
Distinguish between needs and wants.			●	●		
Describe the relationship of price to supply and demand.				●		
Use economic concepts such as supply, demand, and price.			●		●	
Identify examples of private and public goods and services.			●	●	●	
Understand a price is what people pay when they buy a good or service and what they receive when they sell a good or service.			●	●	●	
Interpret, use, and distinguish various representations of the earth, such as maps, globes, and photographs.						●
Use appropriate resources such as atlases, graphs, and maps to interpret information.						●

Unit Overview

Catch a Clue

Objectives

Children will

✓ be introduced to key concepts and vocabulary *before* reading

✓ be able to transfer this key strategy to improve test-taking skills

Implementation

Children will use clues and the process of elimination to predict what the nonfiction reading selection will be about. Copy this page on an overhead transparency, and use it for a whole-class activity. Begin by reading aloud each word, and ask children to repeat the words. Read the clues one at a time. Then, discuss with the class what topic(s) could be eliminated and the reasons why. (Note: There will be clues that do not eliminate any topics. The purpose of this is to teach children that although there is information listed, it is not always helpful information.) Cross off a topic when the class decides that it does not fit the clues. If there is more than one topic left after the class discusses all of the clues, this becomes a prediction activity. When this occurs, reread the clues with the class, and discuss which answer would be most appropriate given the clues provided.

Concept Map

Objectives

Children will

✓ access prior knowledge by brainstorming what they already know about the topic

✓ increase familiarity with the social studies content by hearing others' prior knowledge experiences

✓ revisit the map *after* reading to recall information from the reading selection

Implementation

Copy this page on an overhead transparency, and use it for a whole-class activity. Use a colored pen to write children's prior knowledge on the transparency. After the class reads the story, use a different colored pen to add what children learned.

Word Warm-Up

Objectives

Children will

✓ be introduced to new vocabulary words

✓ make predictions about the story using thinking and reasoning skills

✓ begin to monitor their own comprehension

Implementation

Children will use the strategy of exclusion brainstorming to identify which words are likely to be in the story and which words are unrelated and should be eliminated from the list. Copy this page on an overhead transparency, and use it for a whole-class activity. Have children make predictions about which of the vocabulary words could be in the story and which words probably would not be in the story. Ask them to give reasons for their predictions. For example, say *Do you think the hospital would be in a story about community helpers?* A child may say *Yes, because there are doctors and nurses there to help* or *No, because that is a place to go if you are sick.* Circle the word if a child says that it will be in the story, and cross it out if a child says it will not be in the story. Do not correct children's responses. After reading, children can either confirm or disconfirm their own predictions. It is more powerful for children to verify their predictions on their own than to be told the answer before ever reading the story.

Nonfiction Text

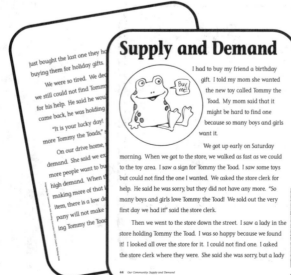

The Story

Objectives

Children will

✓ read high-interest, nonfiction stories

✓ increase social studies knowledge

✓ increase content area vocabulary

✓ connect social studies facts with their own experiences

Implementation

Give each child a copy of the story, and display the corresponding Word Warm-Up transparency while you read the story with the class. After the class reads the story, go back to the transparency, and have children discuss their predictions in relation to the new information they learned in the story. Invite children to identify any changes they would make on the transparency and give reasons for their responses. Then, revisit the corresponding Concept Map transparency, and write the new information children have learned.

Comprehension Questions

Objectives

Children will

✓ recall factual information

✓ be challenged to think beyond the story facts to make inferences

✓ connect the story to other reading, their own lives, and the world around them

Implementation

Use these questions to facilitate a class discussion of the story. Choose the number and types of questions that best meet the abilities of your class.

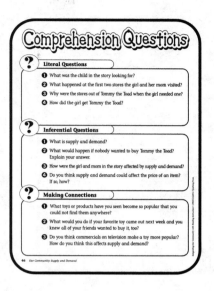

Sharpen Your Skills

Objectives

Children will

✓ practice answering questions in common test-taking formats

✓ integrate language arts skills with social studies knowledge

Implementation

After the class reads a story, give each child a copy of this page. Ask children to read each question and all of the answer choices for that question before deciding on an answer. Show them how to use their pencil to completely fill in the circle for their answer. Invite children to raise their hand if they have difficulty reading a question and/or the answer choices. Thoroughly explain the types of questions and exactly what is being asked the first few times children use this reproducible.

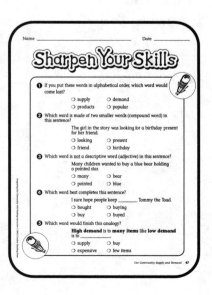

Get Logical

Objectives

Children will

✓ practice logical and strategic thinking skills

✓ practice the skill of process of elimination

✓ transfer the information read by applying it to new situations

Implementation

Give each child a copy of this page. Read the beginning sentences and the clues to familiarize children with the words. Show children step-by-step how to eliminate choices based on the clues given. Have children place an X in a box that represents an impossible choice, thereby narrowing down the options for accurate choices. Once children understand the concept, they can work independently on this reproducible.

Hands-on Social Studies

Social Studies Activity

Objectives

Children will

✓ participate in hands-on learning experiences

✓ expand and reinforce social studies knowledge

✓ apply new social studies vocabulary words

Implementation

The social studies activities in this book incorporate a variety of skills children are required to experience at this age level (e.g., survey, interview, analyze, evaluate). Each hands-on activity begins with an explanation of its purpose to help direct the intended learning. Give each child a copy of any corresponding reproducibles and/or materials for the activity. Then, introduce the activity and explain the directions. Model any directions that may be difficult for children to follow on their own.

Catch a Clue

What will we learn about in our reading today?

community helpers

banks

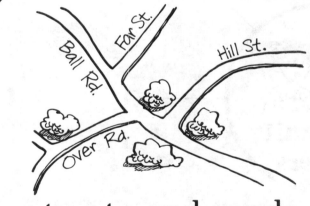

streets and roads

maps

Our Clues

❶ They can be in your **neighborhood**.

❷ They involve people.

❸ They are important to all **communities**.

❹ You might be this someday.

Concept Map

Facts we already know about **community helpers,** and the new facts we have learned

Community Helpers

Integrating Our Community with Reading Instruction © 2002 Creative Teaching Press

Word Warm-Up

Which words might you expect to find in a story about **community helpers?**

firefighter	neighborhood	bikes
hospital	trash cans	teacher
plant	emergency	officer
protects	librarian	dog

Community Helpers

I made a new friend today! Her name is Liz. She just moved in next door. We rode our bikes around town and saw many important places.

The first place we saw was the hospital. I told her that if she gets very sick or hurt, this is where she should go. Nurses and doctors work at the hospital. I told her about the time I fell off my bike and broke my arm. The nurses and doctors were nice to me. They put a cast on my arm. They told us how important it was to only go to the hospital in an emergency and not just for a common cold. This way the people who need care badly will be helped right away.

As we rode on, we heard a siren. It came from the fire station. We saw a fire truck pull out of the driveway. There was a firefighter who stayed behind. We asked him where the fire truck was going. He said there was a fire on a hill. The firefighters went to put out the fire. Firefighters do more than put out fires. They help if there is a car crash. They also teach children about fire safety.

We decided to ride to the park. On our way, we heard a siren. It was a police car going to the fire. We stopped our bikes as the car drove past us. I had seen that same police officer before. She came to my school to teach us about safety! She had told us that she helps the community in many ways. She protects people from crime. She makes sure all people follow the laws. And, she helps people when they are in danger.

We rode to our school next. I told Liz about my teacher. She is very nice and smart. She teaches us math and how to read and write. Some days I help her after school.

As Liz and I rode home, we talked about all the places and people we saw. We felt happy that there were so many people who help our community. Can you think of any other community helpers who might be in your town?

Integrating Our Community with Reading Instruction © 2002 Creative Teaching Press

Comprehension Questions

Integrating Our Community with Reading Instruction © 2002 Creative Teaching Press

? ## Literal Questions

1. In what ways do firefighters help the community?
2. In what ways do nurses and doctors help the community?
3. In what ways do police officers help the community?
4. In what ways do teachers help the community?

? ## Inferential Questions

1. What would happen if your town did not have any police officers or firefighters?
2. Why is it important to thank the community helpers for their hard work?
3. In the story, why were the two children riding around the neighborhood?
4. What is a community helper?

? ## Making Connections

1. Which community job would you be interested in when you grow up? Why?
2. Which community helper do you see the most in your town? What does he or she do? Why is that important?
3. How could you thank community helpers for their hard work?

Sharpen Your Skills

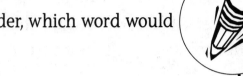

1 If you put these words in alphabetical order, which word would come second?

　　　○ nurse 　　　　○ police

　　　○ doctor 　　　　○ garbage collector

2 What kind of word is "firefighters" in this sentence?

　　　The **firefighters** went to put out the fire.

　　　○ contraction 　　○ compound word

　　　○ adjective 　　　○ verb

3 Which word best completes this sentence?

　　　On our bike tour, we _____ many important places.

　　　○ seen 　　　　○ sawn

　　　○ saw 　　　　○ sawed

4 What punctuation mark should go at the end of this sentence:

　　　Mail carriers are helpers in every community

　　　○ period (.) 　　　○ exclamation point (!)

　　　○ question mark (?) 　○ none of these choices

5 Which word would finish this analogy?

　　　Nurses are to **care for the sick** like **firefighters** are to _____.

　　　○ empty trash bins 　○ deliver the mail

　　　○ fight crime 　　　○ put out fires

Get Logical

Liz and her new friend saw many community helpers on their ride in the neighborhood. Krista, Marco, and Javier each have a parent who is a community helper. Use the clues below to decide what each child's parent does to help others.

Clues

1 Marco's mom helps children find good books for reports.

2 Krista's dad helps children get across the street safely.

3 Javier's mom helps the animals in his town. If they are sick, then she tries to make them better.

	Krista's dad	Marco's mom	Javier's mom
Veterinarian			
Crossing Guard			
Librarian			

Krista's dad is a _____.

Marco's mom is a _____.

Javier's mom is a _____.

Integrating Our Community with Reading Instruction © 2002 Creative Teaching Press

Community Helpers Word Sort

Purpose

The purpose of this activity is for children to critically analyze community helpers and the services they provide. The purpose of the follow-up activity is for children to write a thank-you letter to a community helper.

MATERIALS

✔ Community Helpers Word Sort (page 18)

Implementation

After teaching about community jobs, give each child a Community Helpers Word Sort. Read aloud with children the job descriptions in the boxes at the top of the page and the job titles in the boxes below. Have children read one description at a time and then decide which job title or titles it matches. Show children how to write the number of the job description in the box or boxes with the correct job title. (Note that there will be more than one description for each job title.) Then, tell them to cross out each description. When children have completed their word sorts, review the page with the whole class. Read aloud a description, and invite a child to tell you which job title(s) he or she chose for it. Ask children to explain their reasons for choosing a particular answer. As a follow-up to this activity, have children write a thank-you letter to a community helper in their community. Invite children to draw a picture to include with the letter.

Name _____   Date _____

Community Helpers Word Sort

Directions: Read one job description at a time. Decide which worker or workers would do the task at his or her job. Then, write the number for that phrase in the box or boxes with the correct job title. Cross out each description as you go.

1 Gives people shots	**2** Delivers mail	**3** Collects trash	**4** Keeps money safe
5 Gives people medicine	**6** Helps you find books	**7** Drives children safely	**8** Helps with accidents
9 Turns on electricity	**10** Puts out fires	**11** Teaches about safety	**12** Helps enforce laws
13 Gives people stamps	**14** Helps your pets	**15** Fixes street lights	**16** Helps animals feel better
17 Blocks traffic	**18** Helps you do research	**19** Takes your temperature	**20** Brings kids to school
21 Cashes checks	**22** Gives tickets	**23** Gives pets medicine	**24** Helps at school

Nurse	Doctor	Postal Worker	Trash Collector
Banker	**Firefighter**	**Police Officer**	**Crossing Guard**
Electric Company Worker	**Veterinarian**	**Librarian**	**Bus Driver**

Integrating Our Community with Reading Instruction © 2002 Creative Teaching Press

Catch a Clue

What will we learn about in our reading today?

good citizens

inventors

community helpers

astronauts

Our Clues

❶ We will be learning about people.

❷ They are helpful people.

❸ You can be one of these people right now.

❹ We should all try to be one every day.

Concept Map

Facts we already know about **good citizens**, and the new facts we have learned

Integrating Our Community with Reading Instruction © 2002 Creative Teaching Press

Word Warm-Up

Which words might you expect to find in a story about **good citizens?**

kind	help	respect
listens	trip	responsible
caring	community	share
homework	fair	state

Good Citizens

What is a citizen? A citizen is a member of a community. A community is a group of people. A community can have a lot of people or not very many people. Do you belong to any communities?

Do you think about what will make other people happy? A good citizen thinks about all people. How can you be a good citizen? You can treat others the way you want them to treat you. Some people call this the "Golden Rule." You can play fair. You can be kind to others. You can help other people. You can be a good sport. Would you like to meet some boys and girls who are good citizens?

Meet Jill. Jill is a good citizen on the playground each day. One day, she was playing a game. There was a problem. One person made up all of the rules. Jill said that each person should get to vote on the rules. This made the game more fair. All of the boys and girls were happy.

Integrating Our Community with Reading Instruction © 2002 Creative Teaching Press

Meet Dan. Dan is a good citizen in the classroom. He raises his hand when he wants to talk. He tries not to talk while his teacher is talking. He listens to what other people have to say. Dan shows respect when he does these things. Dan likes to say nice things to other people. He also likes to do nice things for other people. One time, his friend Tom did not have a pencil. Dan gave Tom one of his. Dan always tries to share, be kind, and show respect to all people.

Meet Kim. Kim is a good citizen at home. When she comes home from school, she does her chores right away. Her dad does not have to ask her to do them. Then she does her homework. She always does her best on her work. If she makes a mess, Kim cleans it up each time. Kim likes to be responsible.

Do you play fair? Are you responsible? Do you treat other people the way you want them to treat you? If so, then you are a good citizen!

Comprehension Questions

? Literal Questions

❶ What is a citizen?

❷ What is a community?

❸ How was Dan a good citizen?

❹ How was Kim a good citizen?

? Inferential Questions

❶ Why is it important to be a good citizen?

❷ How would life be different at your school if the children in your class were not good citizens?

❸ Sam does not raise his hand. He throws his napkin on the ground. He will not share the ball. Is Sam acting like a good citizen? Explain your answer.

❹ Why is it respectful not to talk when other people are talking?

? Making Connections

❶ Good citizens are not perfect people. They just try their best to make good choices. Are you a good citizen? Give reasons to explain your answer.

❷ Are your friends good citizens? Give reasons to explain your answer.

❸ What can you do to be a better citizen at school and at home?

Integrating Our Community with Reading Instruction © 2002 Creative Teaching Press

Name _____   Date _____

Sharpen Your Skills

1 If you put these words in alphabetical order, which word would come first?

    ○ citizen   ○ responsible

    ○ respect   ○ fair

2 What two words make up the contraction "wouldn't" in this sentence?

Good citizens **wouldn't** have friends if they didn't try to be kind to others.

    ○ will not   ○ would not

    ○ should not   ○ did not

3 Which word is an action word (verb) in this sentence?

Molly shared her new birthday game with her little sister.

    ○ birthday   ○ little

    ○ sister   ○ shared

4 Which word needs a capital letter in this sentence?

good citizens are kind to other people.

    ○ people   ○ good

    ○ kind   ○ citizens

5 Which word would finish this analogy?

Good citizen is to **helpful** like **not a good citizen** is to _____.

    ○ respectful   ○ nice

    ○ fair   ○ unkind

Name _____   Date _____

Get Logical

Good citizens are responsible, respectful, and fair. Keith, Sandy, and Kendra are all good citizens. Each person tries his or her best in one of these areas. Use the clues below to decide how each person tries his or her best to be a good citizen.

Clues

1 Kendra sees some friends on the playground. One friend is telling everyone else what to do. Kendra helps them agree to take turns.

2 Keith says "please" and "thank you" all the time. He opens the car door for his mom.

3 Sandy feeds her pet rabbit every day and changes its water.

	Keith	Sandy	Kendra
Be Responsible			
Show Respect			
Be Fair			

Keith tries hard to _____.

Sandy tries hard to _____.

Kendra tries hard to _____.

Integrating Our Community with Reading Instruction © 2002 Creative Teaching Press

Good Citizens Survey

Purpose

The purpose of this activity is for children to recognize what character traits are associated with good citizens; interview people; and practice collecting, compiling, and analyzing data.

Implementation

Give each child a Good Citizens Survey. Read aloud the questions and answer choices on the survey. Explain to children how to interview another person using the survey. Model for children how to ask another child a question, wait for his or her response, and circle the answer on the survey paper. Next, divide the class into pairs and have children survey their partner. (Be sure no children interview the same child. If you have more than one child interview the same child, it will skew the results.) Then, copy The Survey Says reproducible on an overhead transparency. Use this page to record, analyze, and discuss the results of the surveys with your class. Read aloud each question. For each answer choice, have children raise their hand if their partner chose that answer. Use tally marks to record the survey results in the boxes on the transparency. Total the tally marks for the responses to each question, and record each number in the appropriate box. Discuss the questions at the bottom of the page, and record the answers. Brainstorm with children what characteristics they think represent a good citizen, and list their responses on the chalkboard. To extend the activity, have your class interview additional classes, and compile all of the data on the transparency. Also, remind children to feel proud that they are at a great school with lots of good citizens!

Data collected by: _____

Citizen who was interviewed: _____

Good Citizens Survey

Directions: Read each question and its choices to the person you are interviewing. Tell the person to pick the answer that says what he or she thinks a good citizen would do. Circle the letter for his or her answer.

1 If you saw someone fall down during recess, what would you do?

    a. help the person   **b.** go play   **c.** laugh at the person

2 If you found a $5.00 bill on the ground, what would you do?

    a. keep it   **b.** look for the owner and then keep it   **c.** take it to the lost and found

3 If you wanted to tell your mom something but she was on the phone, what would you do?

    a. throw a fit   **b.** write a note to show her   **c.** hang up the phone on her

4 If you were playing your favorite game and your dad told you to go do your homework, what would you do?

    a. keep playing the game   **b.** put the game away   **c.** ask him to play with you

5 What do you think a good citizen would <u>not</u> do?

    a. pick up trash off the street   **b.** help others   **c.** steal

Integrating Our Community with Reading Instruction © 2002 Creative Teaching Press

The Survey Says

Total Number of People Surveyed: _____

Question Number	Answer "a"	Answer "b"	Answer "c"
1			
2			
3			
4			
5			

❶ For each question, which answer had the most responses?

_____

❷ For each question, which answer had the least responses?

_____

❸ Were there any answers that were not chosen? _____ If so, which ones?

_____

❹ Looking separately at each answer that was not chosen, discuss why you think it was not chosen.

_____

❺ What characteristics do you think a good citizen would have?

_____

Integrating Our Community with Reading Instruction © 2002 Creative Teaching Press

Catch a Clue

money

the library

education

family

Our clues

❶ You probably see it every day.

❷ You need to work hard to get it.

❸ You need to make smart choices with it.

❹ You can save it or spend it.

Concept Map

Facts we already know about **responsible spending,** and the new facts we have learned

Responsible Spending

Word Warm-Up

Which words might you expect to find in a story about **responsible spending?**

account	scooter	allowance
responsible	future	learned
patient	bathroom	earn
bank	smart	chair

Responsible Spending

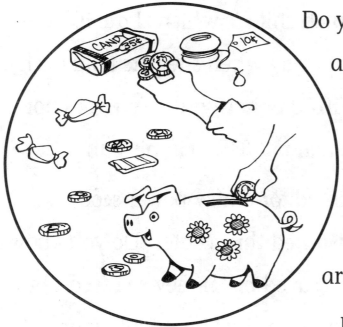

Do you make money by doing chores at home? Do you get money for your birthdays? What do you do with your money? If you save it, then you are a saver. If you spend it right away, then you are a spender. Which one are you?

Pretend that the Smith family lives next door to you. Mr. Smith works in a store. He works hard to earn his money. Mrs. Smith is a teacher. She works hard to earn her money. Kate and Ken are Mr. and Mrs. Smith's children. They get money from their parents when they do their chores. They both get $10.00 a week for an allowance. Each day, Kate makes her bed, takes out the trash, and sets the table. She works hard to earn her money. Her brother, Ken, feeds the dog, mows the lawn, and cleans the bathroom. He works hard to earn his money.

Kate and Ken each have a piggy bank. One bank is almost full. One bank is almost empty. One child is a spender and one is

Integrating Our Community with Reading Instruction © 2002 Creative Teaching Press

a saver. Let's see if you can tell which child is which. Kate likes to spend her money at the store right away when she gets paid each week. In one month, Kate saved $10.00 in her bank. Ken does not buy candy or toys. In one month, Ken put $35.00 in his bank.

One day, Kate and Ken saw an ad for a new power scooter. The price was $25.00. They both wanted this scooter. Do you know who can buy it? That is right! Ken saved his money so he can buy the scooter now. He had thought that one day he might want to buy something really special. He did not want to use his money on little things. It was hard for him when he saw Kate eating candy and playing with new small toys each week! But Ken thought about the future. Ken wanted to have enough money to buy a great toy when it came along.

How do you think Kate felt? Kate was mad and sad. She wanted a power scooter, too. She did not have enough money to buy it. She did not get one. She learned that she will have to save her money. How smart are you with money?

Integrating Our Community with Reading Instruction © 2002 Creative Teaching Press

Comprehension Questions

Literal Questions

1. What is an allowance? How did Kate and Ken get one?

2. What is the difference between a saver and a spender?

3. Name three things that Ken had to do in order to have enough money to buy a terrific toy.

4. Was Kate a saver or spender? How do you know?

Inferential Questions

1. Do you think it is better to be a saver or a spender? Why?

2. Name three things that could happen if Mr. and Mrs. Smith always spent all of their money after they earned it.

3. How does someone become a saver?

4. Pretend that you have a friend who is a big spender. Give your friend three suggestions so he can learn how to save more money.

Making Connections

1. Are you more of a saver or a spender? How do you know?

2. Ask your parents if they are savers or spenders. Have them help you make a list of things they are saving up for.

3. Set some goals for yourself. Write down how much you want to save, by what date, and what you are saving it for.

Integrating Our Community with Reading Instruction © 2002 Creative Teaching Press

Sharpen Your Skills

1 If you put these words in alphabetical order, which word would come first?

- ○ saver
- ○ future
- ○ spender
- ○ allowance

2 How many sentences are in this paragraph?

If you really want to save some money for your future, then you should ask your parents to open a savings account for you at a bank. Your money can earn even more money at the bank. That is being "money smart"!

- ○ one
- ○ three
- ○ two
- ○ four

3 Which word is a descriptive word (adjective) in this sentence?

If you are a smart saver, then you will have money when you need it.

- ○ money
- ○ smart
- ○ saver
- ○ have

4 Which word best completes this sentence?

Ken listened to his parents and _____ for his future.

- ○ saved
- ○ save
- ○ saving
- ○ savered

5 Which word would finish this analogy?

Spending is to **fun** like _____ is to **smart**.

- ○ wasting
- ○ throwing
- ○ saving
- ○ buying

Integrating Our Community with Reading Instruction © 2002 Creative Teaching Press

Get Logical

Lina, Mario, and LaTeisha are all trying to be "money smart." They each listed goals and created a plan to save more money. Use the clues below to decide what each child is doing to save more money.

Clues

1 The person who put money in envelopes was not LaTeisha.

2 The person who stopped spending money every day was not Mario.

3 Mario thought that if he could see his money, then he would spend it. He had to put it in a safe place. Now he cannot get his money without his parents. He has saved a lot of money.

	Lina	Mario	LaTeisha
Puts money in a savings account at the bank			
Puts weekly allowance into an envelope and seals it			
Buys something every other day instead of every day			

Lina _____.

Mario _____.

LaTeisha _____.

Integrating Our Community with Reading Instruction © 2002 Creative Teaching Press

Money Smart or Money Foolish?

Purpose

The purpose of this activity is to give children practice making good money choices and to instill in them a greater appreciation for being a responsible spender.

Integrating *Our Community with Reading Instruction* © 2002 Creative Teaching Press

MATERIALS

- ✔ Money Mittens reproducible (page 39)
- ✔ Money Smart Scenarios reproducible (page 40)
- ✔ construction paper
- ✔ crayons or markers
- ✔ scissors
- ✔ tape
- ✔ craft sticks

Implementation

Copy the Money Mittens reproducible on construction paper for each child. Have children color their mittens and then cut them out. Tape a craft stick to each mitten. Read aloud the Money Smart Scenarios one at a time. Give children a chance to think about each scenario and form their own opinion. Ask children *Is it money smart or money foolish?* Tell them to raise one of their "money mittens" to indicate their answer. After the class votes on each scenario, discuss that situation. Ask children to explain their answer. After you have read the money smart scenarios and children have voted on them, invite children to share a scenario of their own for others to vote on. Remind children that they should not be swayed by their classmates' opinions. Explain how important it is to have one's own opinion. Note that even if several children vote one way, another child may still have a good reason for taking the opposing opinion.

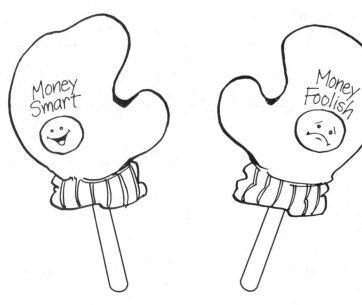

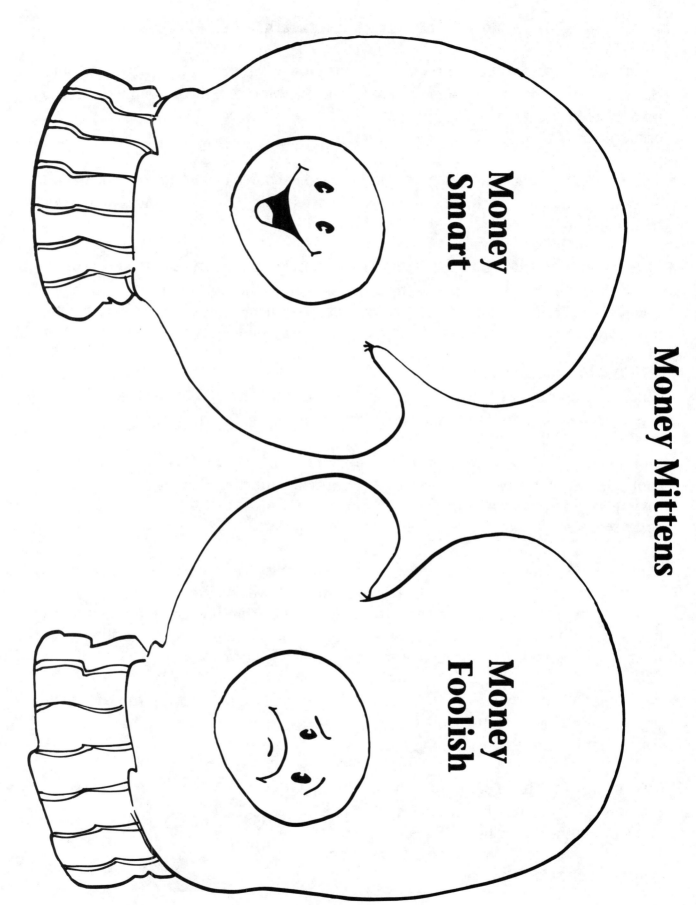

Money Mittens

Money
Smart

Money
Foolish

Integrating Our Community with Reading Instruction © 2002 Creative Teaching Press

Money Smart Scenarios

◆ Johnny has a piggy bank in his room. He is trying to save his money for a new dictionary. His friend wants him to buy some candy for them to eat after school. Johnny decides to take the money out of his piggy bank and buy some candy bars. Was this money smart or money foolish?

◆ Sally gets $5.00 in allowance each week if she does her chores. Every Saturday, she spends $4.75 at the toy store on the stuffed bears that she is collecting. Is this money smart or money foolish?

◆ Brittany collects soda cans in her house in a special trash can. At the end of each month, she smashes the cans, bags them, and goes with her dad to the recycling center. The people at the recycling center give her money for her cans and thank her for helping the earth. She spends all of the money right away on toys. Is this money smart or money foolish?

◆ Charlene wants to buy a new purse. It costs $12.00. She has $4.00. She makes a plan to save all of her allowance until she has $12.00. Is this money smart or money foolish?

◆ Marcy just got $100.00 for her birthday from her uncle. She wants to buy a new remote controlled car. It will cost all of her money. She decides to put half of the money into her savings account and wait until she saves more money to get the car. She thinks it might go on sale someday, too. Is this money smart or money foolish?

◆ Ophelia has a deal with her mom. If she cuts out coupons from the paper and keeps them organized, then she can have any money that is saved on the grocery bill. Ophelia gets a recipe box and sorts the coupons by food group. She shops with her mom and always saves her mom at least $10.00. Ophelia puts all of the money in a lock box. Her mom has the only key. Is this money smart or money foolish?

◆ Peter and Polly are twins. They want to get their parents a new picture frame for their anniversary. They save their allowance for two weeks and put it together to buy a frame. Is this money smart or money foolish?

◆ Vincent saw that his mom did not have enough money to pay the bills. He went to his piggy bank and took out the money he had saved. He gave it to his mom so she could pay the bills. Is this money smart or money foolish?

Integrating Our Community with Reading Instruction © 2002 Creative Teaching Press

Catch a Clue

Integrating Our Community with Reading Instruction © 2002 Creative Teaching Press

What will we learn about in our reading today?

money

supply and demand

banks

life long ago

Our Clues

❶ We will talk about spending money.

❷ This is all around us.

❸ This involves things being made.

❹ If more of something is wanted, then more is created.

Concept Map

Facts we already know about **supply and demand**, and the new facts we have learned

Supply and Demand

Integrating Our Community with Reading Instruction © 2002 Creative Teaching Press

Word Warm-Up

Tulips $0.35 each

Roses $1.00 each

Carnations $0.10 each

Which words might you expect to find in a story about **supply and demand?**

holiday	company	empty
store	cost	helpful
clerk	telephone	truck
buying	toys	people

Supply and Demand

I had to buy my friend a birthday gift. I told my mom she wanted the new toy called Tommy the Toad. My mom said that it might be hard to find one because so many boys and girls want it.

We got up early on Saturday morning. When we got to the store, we walked as fast as we could to the toy area. I saw a sign for Tommy the Toad. I saw some toys but could not find the one I wanted. We asked the store clerk for help. He said he was sorry, but they did not have any more. "So many boys and girls love Tommy the Toad! We sold out the very first day we had it!" said the store clerk.

Then we went to the store down the street. I saw a lady in the store holding Tommy the Toad. I was so happy because we found it! I looked all over the store for it. I could not find one. I asked the store clerk where they were. She said she was sorry, but a lady

Integrating Our Community with Reading Instruction © 2002 Creative Teaching Press

just bought the last one they had. She said so many people were buying them for holiday gifts.

We were so tired. We decided to try one more store. Again, we still could not find Tommy the Toad. We asked the store clerk for his help. He said he would look in the back for one. When he came back, he was holding the toy we wanted! I was so happy!

"It is your lucky day! A truck just pulled up and brought us more Tommy the Toads," said the store clerk as he gave it to me.

On our drive home, my mom told me about supply and demand. She said we experienced it today. She said that when more people want to buy something like Tommy the Toad, there is a high demand. When there is a high demand, a company will keep making more of that item. But, when not many people want an item, there is a low demand. When there is a low demand, a company will not make many of the item. I sure hope people keep buying Tommy the Toad. I do not want companies to stop making them!

Integrating Our Community with Reading Instruction © 2002 Creative Teaching Press

Comprehension Questions

? Literal Questions

1. What was the child in the story looking for?

2. What happened at the first two stores the girl and her mom visited?

3. Why were the stores out of Tommy the Toad when the girl needed one?

4. How did the girl get Tommy the Toad?

? Inferential Questions

1. What is supply and demand?

2. What would happen if nobody wanted to buy Tommy the Toad? Explain your answer.

3. How were the girl and mom in the story affected by supply and demand?

4. Do you think supply and demand could affect the price of an item? If so, how?

? Making Connections

1. What toys or products have you seen become so popular that you could not find them anywhere?

2. What would you do if your favorite toy came out next week and you knew all of your friends wanted to buy it, too?

3. Do you think commercials on television make a toy more popular? How do you think this affects supply and demand?

Integrating Our Community with Reading Instruction © 2002 Creative Teaching Press

Sharpen Your Skills

1 If you put these words in alphabetical order, which word would come last?

○ supply   ○ demand

○ products   ○ popular

2 Which word is made of two smaller words (compound word) in this sentence?

The girl in the story was looking for a birthday present for her friend.

○ looking   ○ present

○ friend   ○ birthday

3 Which word is <u>not</u> a descriptive word (adjective) in this sentence?

Many children wanted to buy a blue bear holding a pointed star.

○ many   ○ bear

○ pointed   ○ blue

4 Which word best completes this sentence?

I sure hope people keep _____ Tommy the Toad.

○ bought   ○ buying

○ buy   ○ buyed

5 Which word would finish this analogy?

High demand is to **many items** like **low demand** is to _____.

○ supply   ○ buy

○ expensive   ○ few items

Integrating Our Community with Reading Instruction © 2002 Creative Teaching Press

Get Logical

The Supersize Pet Store sells different breeds of dogs. There are **7 golden retrievers, 3 boxers, and 1 bichon frise** in the store. Miguel, Hannah, and Ronald are each at the store to buy a dog. Use this information and the clues below to decide which breed of dog each child wants to buy.

Clues

1. The pet store has a large supply of the kind of dog Hannah wants.

2. Miguel wants a rare breed. He will have to wait three months to get one because the store already sold the one it had.

3. Ronald is at the pet store to buy a breed of dog that is available. He does not have as many to choose from as Hannah does.

	Miguel	Hannah	Ronald
Bichon Frise			
Golden Retriever			
Boxer			

Miguel wants a _____.

Hannah wants a _____.

Ronald wants a _____.

Snack Shop Shopping Spree

Purpose

The purpose of this activity is for children to gain a better understanding of the concepts of consumer finance and supply and demand. It will also help them to see how supply and demand affects what people are able to buy.

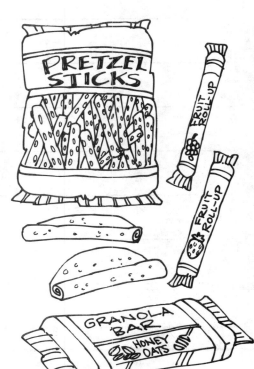

Implementation

In advance, post outside the classroom door the Shopping Spree Snack List, which asks parents to donate specific food items. If parents in your school community cannot donate any items, then use it as a shopping list. Also, ask for parent volunteers to help on the day of the shopping spree, or enlist an upper-grade classroom to help you. Put $1.00 in coins in a separate plastic bag for each child. Make a copy of the Shopping Spree Record for each child.

On the day of your shopping spree, set up the various food items at different "stations" in the room. Have one volunteer at each station to collect money and give out the snacks. Give each child a Shopping Spree Record and a bag of money. Have children mark an X under the "I want it" column for each item they would like to buy. Then, invite children to walk to different stations to buy the foods they want. Show them how to record each purchase on their recording sheet as well as how to circle whether or not the supply and demand of each item was high or low. (Have the volunteer at each station assist children in recording the information.) As the children shop, they will begin to discover that they cannot buy everything they want. When children are finished, discuss which snacks disappeared first and why. Ask such questions as *Was there enough supply? What was the demand for each product? What would you need to do next time to make sure that everyone was able to buy the items that they really wanted? Why couldn't you buy some of the items you wanted this time? How did the supply and demand affect what you were able to buy? How did the price affect the supply or demand?*

Shopping Spree Snack List

Our class is learning about the concept of supply and demand. To give children a greater understanding of this concept, we are completing an activity called the Snack Shop Shopping Spree. The items listed below are necessary to complete the activity. If you are able to donate any of these items, our class would greatly appreciate it. Please sign your name next to an item you would like to donate. Please bring the item you are donating to school by _____. Thank you for helping us learn a valuable lesson!

Item	Quantity	Name of Donor
Baby Carrots	2 small bags	
Large Pretzel Sticks	1 bag	
Cookies	1 package	
Frosted Cupcakes	12	
Celery	1 stalk cut in half	
Candy Bars	8 bars	
Licorice	2 packages	
Shelled Peanuts	1 package	
Fruit Roll-Ups®	6 servings	
Small Fruit	10 servings	
Granola Bars	1 box	
Lemonade	1 carton	

Name _____   Date _____

Shopping Spree Record

Directions: You have $1.00 to spend. Mark an X under the "I want it" column for each item you would like to buy. Walk to different food stations to buy these items. Then, mark an X under the "I bought it" column for each item you bought. Write in the amount you spent and circle whether the supply and demand were high or low. Have fun!

Item	I want it	I bought it	It costs	I spent	Supply	Demand
Carrot	☐	☐	5¢	_____	high/low	high/low
Pretzel	☐	☐	15¢	_____	high/low	high/low
Cookie	☐	☐	65¢	_____	high/low	high/low
Cupcake	☐	☐	80¢	_____	high/low	high/low
Celery	☐	☐	10¢	_____	high/low	high/low
Candy Bar	☐	☐	85¢	_____	high/low	high/low
Licorice	☐	☐	20¢	_____	high/low	high/low
Peanut	☐	☐	15¢	_____	high/low	high/low
Fruit Roll-Up®	☐	☐	55¢	_____	high/low	high/low
Fruit	☐	☐	40¢	_____	high/low	high/low
Granola Bar	☐	☐	30¢	_____	high/low	high/low
Lemonade	☐	☐	35¢	_____	high/low	high/low

I bought _____ snacks. They cost me _____. I have _____ left. The most popular item was _____. The supply was _____ for this item. The demand was _____ for this item. We needed _____ of it. Next time, we need to _____ to have enough of it for everyone who wants to buy it.

Catch a Clue

What will we learn about in our reading today?

helping in the community

starting your own business

making responsible choices

making friends

Our Clues

❶ You can do it.

❷ You can help other people.

❸ You need to be organized.

❹ You can earn money.

Concept Map

Facts we already know about **kids in business,** and the new facts we have learned

Kids in Business

Word Warm-Up

Which words might you expect to find in a story about **kids in business?**

customers	cats	charge
bank	donate	money
hospital	mayor	organized
store	supplies	raise

Integrating Our Community with Reading Instruction © 2002 Creative Teaching Press

Kids in Business

Do you like to be in charge? Do you like to make things? Do you like to sell things? Do you like helping other people? Do you have great ideas? Did you say yes to any of these questions? Then, you might want to start your own business. You can. It is easy. Kids just like you are doing great things to help others.

Last weekend, Pam and John saw a show on TV. It was about kids helping other kids. They saw some kids with illnesses in a hospital. They looked sad. Pam and John wanted to make them feel better.

Pam and John had a great idea. They would sell lemonade. They told their parents about their idea. They went to the store. They bought lemonade, cups, and napkins. The supplies cost $10.00. They made a big sign that told people the money would go to the kids in the hospital. They started their own business the

Integrating Our Community with Reading Instruction © 2002 Creative Teaching Press

next weekend. They sold the lemonade on their street corner with their parents. They sold many cups of lemonade. They could have sold more lemonade if they had not run out of supplies.

Pam and John's business plan worked! At the end of the day, Pam and John had $45.00 to help the kids in the hospital. First, Pam and John paid back their mom and dad the $10.00 they used for supplies to open their business. They used the rest of the money to buy games, toys, and books. Pam and John's parents took them to donate the gifts to the hospital. They made many kids feel happy by their act of kindness.

What business would you like to start? First, you need to think about why you want to raise money. Then, you need to think about what you can do. Then, you need a plan. What supplies would you need? How much will you charge? Do you need help? What will you do with the money? These are just a few things to think about before you start your own business. Oh, and don't forget to have fun!

Integrating Our Community with Reading Instruction © 2002 Creative Teaching Press

Comprehension Questions

?

Literal Questions

1. What business did Pam and John begin?

2. What did Pam and John do with the money they earned?

3. What questions do you need to think about before starting your own business?

4. How could Pam and John have made more money selling lemonade?

Inferential Questions

1. What do you think is included in a business plan?

2. Why do you think it is important to think about what you need, how much you will charge, and who will help you before you open a business?

3. How much money did Pam and John have to spend on gifts?

4. How do you think most businesses get started?

Making Connections

1. What business would you like to start? Who would work for you? How would you advertise? What would you do? How much would you charge?

2. Why would you be a good person to start a business?

3. Think of a business of your own. Write a business plan.

Integrating Our Community with Reading Instruction © 2002 Creative Teaching Press

Name _____   Date _____

Sharpen Your Skills

1 If you put these words in alphabetical order, which word would come third?

○ help   ○ give

○ act   ○ think

2 Which word shows more than one person or thing (plural) in this sentence?

Some children sold lemonade to buy gifts.

○ sold   ○ lemonade

○ buy   ○ gifts

3 Which word is an action word (verb) in this sentence?

Pam and John sold lemonade to earn money for the children in the hospital.

○ lemonade   ○ money

○ hospital   ○ sold

4 What punctuation mark should go at the end of this sentence:

What type of business would you want to start someday

○ question mark (?)   ○ period (.)

○ exclamation point (!) ○ none of these choices

5 Which word would finish this analogy?

Owners are to **sell** like _____ are to **buy.**

○ people   ○ sellers

○ children   ○ customers

Integrating Our Community with Reading Instruction © 2002 Creative Teaching Press

Get Logical

Shirleen, Tyrone, and Lucy decided to start a snow shoveling business. First, they needed to make a business plan. Each person had to learn more about and create one important part of the business plan. Use the clues below to decide which part of the business plan each friend organized.

Clues

❶ Lucy was in charge of making coupons and posters. She also put notes in her neighbors' mailboxes.

❷ Shirleen talked to the people who called to have their driveway shoveled. She wrote each person's name and address on paper.

❸ Tyrone was in charge of shopping. He bought shovels, salt, and gloves.

	Shirleen	Tyrone	Lucy
How to advertise			
Who will buy the service			
What they will need			

Shirleen organized _____.

Tyrone organized _____.

Lucy organized _____.

A Busy Business Research Project

Purpose

The purpose of this activity is to provoke children's interest in the businesses of their community, the products and services these businesses provide, and the people who work at them. Children will also experience interviewing a person as a form of research and presenting an oral report.

MATERIALS

✔ A Busy Business reproducible (page 61)

Implementation

Brainstorm with children some of the businesses in their community. List their responses on the chalkboard. Discuss with children what the difference is between a product and a service. Explain that a product is something that can be bought and taken home to use and a service is something someone does for you in return for money. Note that in some cases, a business might do both. Discuss what type of business each is and whether the business sells a product, a service, or both. Write the businesses on a piece of paper with a short note explaining the activity. Make a copy of the note for each child to take home. Have children pick a business that is close to their home to visit with a parent, and ask parents to sign the paper showing their consent to assist with the project. (If parental help is not available, then the school can become that child's business, and he or she can interview the principal.)

Once all of the consent forms are returned, give each child A Busy Business reproducible. Read aloud and discuss each question. Have children take home the form and visit the business. Encourage them to visit the business with a parent, interview the manager or owner of the business, and record what they learned on their form. Ask children to bring the completed form back to school one or two weeks later. Encourage children to make a poster that shows what the business does. Invite children to share the information about the business they visited with the class. When this project is complete, have each child write a thank-you letter to the businessperson he or she interviewed.

Integrating Our Community with Reading Instruction © 2002 Creative Teaching Press

Name _____ Date _____

A Busy Business

Name of the business: _____

Business address: _____

Type of business: _____

Name of the owner or manager you interviewed: _____

Questions to ask the person you interview

❶ Does your business sell a product, a service, or both?

_____

❷ What did you need to do before your business could open?

_____

❸ How do you advertise for your business?

_____

❹ When do you see the highest demand for your product or service? A certain time of day? A certain month or season?

_____

❺ Where do you get your supplies?

_____

❻ Do you make a product here or are products sent to you to sell?

_____

❼ What is one problem your business is trying to solve?

_____

❽ What is your plan for solving this problem?

Thank you for your time! ☺

Integrating Our Community with Reading Instruction © 2002 Creative Teaching Press

Catch a Clue

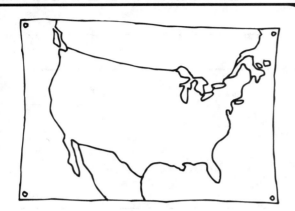

maps

community workers

covered wagons

coins of the world

Our Clues

❶ They help people.

❷ You can buy them in a store.

❸ They come in different shapes and sizes.

❹ You can read them to find your way.

Integrating Our Community with Reading Instruction © 2002 Creative Teaching Press

Concept Map

Facts we already know about **maps,** and the new facts we have learned

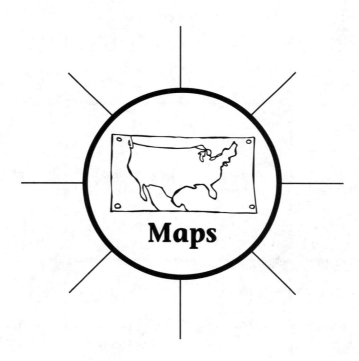

Maps

Word Warm-Up

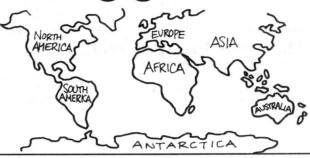

Which words might you expect to find in a story about **maps?**

directions	lost	carnival
cardinal	monkeys	entrance
museum	airport	bedroom
road	south	miles

Integrating Our Community with Reading Instruction © 2002 Creative Teaching Press

Reading a Map

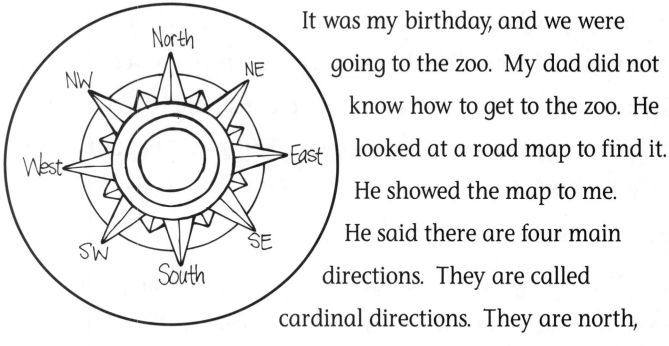

It was my birthday, and we were going to the zoo. My dad did not know how to get to the zoo. He looked at a road map to find it. He showed the map to me. He said there are four main directions. They are called cardinal directions. They are north, south, east, and west. Dad said we would drive five miles south on the freeway. Then, we would drive two miles west to get to the zoo. We got in the car and drove to the zoo.

The people at the zoo gave us a map. My mom said it was to help us find our way at the zoo. My mom asked me what animal I wanted to see. I told her I wanted to see the monkeys.

We had to look on the map to find the monkeys' cage. We saw a box at the bottom of the map. It had pictures and words in it. The same pictures were all over the map. My mom said this key, or legend, would tell us what each picture stood for. She said

Integrating Our Community with Reading Instruction © 2002 Creative Teaching Press

we first needed to find where we were on the map. We found a gate that said "Enter" on the map. This is where we were standing. Then, we saw a picture of a monkey in the legend box. We found the same monkey picture on the map. The map showed the path to walk from where we were to where we wanted to go. We used the map all day. We did not get lost one time!

When we got home, my dad helped me make a map of my bedroom. He told me I needed to pretend I was looking down on my room from the ceiling. He said maps are drawn from this "bird's-eye" view. We drew the things I saw in the room. We also added a legend box. We wrote down the cardinal directions. Then, we used the map for a game. My dad hid a gift in my room. He put an X on the map to show where the gift was. He gave the map to me. I used it to find my gift. I found my gift quickly using the map.

My dad said maps help people get from place to place. He told me there are many different kinds of maps. There are road maps, trail maps, city maps, and many more. You can also get a map to show a larger area like the oceans and continents!

Integrating Our Community with Reading Instruction © 2002 Creative Teaching Press

Comprehension Questions

Literal Questions

❶ What are the four main cardinal directions?

❷ What is a legend on a map?

❸ How did the family in the story find the monkeys?

❹ From what view are maps drawn?

Inferential Questions

❶ Name three different reasons why maps are important.

❷ What might have happened if the dad in the story did not have a map to the zoo?

❸ Why do you think maps are made from a "bird's-eye" view?

❹ Why do you think it is important to have a legend on a map?

Making Connections

❶ Make a map of your bedroom. Label the cardinal directions and items in your room. Look at your map. If you stood at the doorway looking into your room, what direction would you be facing?

❷ Name three places you have been where you have seen maps. Did you use them? Why or why not?

❸ Do you think you could draw a map to represent your classroom? What pictures would you draw to put in the legend? What would they represent?

Sharpen Your Skills

1 If you put these words in alphabetical order, which word would come third?

❍ legend   ❍ map

❍ cardinal   ❍ directions

2 If you were facing north, which direction would be on your right?

❍ north   ❍ south

❍ east   ❍ west

3 Which word is a person, place, or thing (noun) in this sentence?

A map can help people from becoming lost.

❍ help   ❍ lost

❍ map   ❍ none of these choices

4 Which word best completes this sentence?

On a map, the box with pictures and words is called the legend. A legend _____ you the meaning of each picture on the map.

❍ told   ❍ telling

❍ tell   ❍ tells

5 Which word would finish this analogy?

North is to **south** like _____ is to **west**.

❍ east   ❍ south

❍ directions   ❍ southeast

Integrating Our Community with Reading Instruction © 2002 Creative Teaching Press

Get Logical

Kyle, Dylan, and Mary each have a map for their vacation. Use the clues below to decide where each child will visit while on vacation.

Clues

1 The legend on Mary's map has a picture of some tigers and a gorilla.

2 The legend on Dylan's map has a picture of a camera, some fish, a dolphin, and a sea lion.

3 Kyle's map has a legend with a picture of a dinosaur, a covered wagon, and butterflies.

	Kyle	Dylan	Mary
Zoo			
Museum			
Aquarium			

Kyle will visit the _____ while on vacation.

Dylan will visit the _____ while on vacation.

Mary will visit the _____ while on vacation.

Find Your Way Around Bailey Town

Purpose

The purpose of this activity is to get children interested in reading maps, while reinforcing their learning of important parts on a map such as cardinal directions; names of streets, cities, and/or states; and legends.

MATERIALS

✔ Find Your Way Around Bailey Town reproducible (page 71)
✔ Bailey Town Map (page 72)
✔ overhead transparency/ projector

Implementation

Give each child a Find Your Way Around Bailey Town reproducible and a Bailey Town Map. Read aloud each question, and review the cardinal directions and basic outline of the Bailey Town Map with children. Divide the class into small groups. Tell children to read each question and use the map to decide on an answer. Have children write their answers on the lines provided. Make a copy of the Bailey Town Map on an overhead transparency. When children have completed their pages, review each question with the whole class. Invite children to show on the transparency how they found their answers.

Integrating Our Community with Reading Instruction © 2002 Creative Teaching Press

Name _____ Date _____

Find Your Way Around Bailey Town

Directions: Read each question. Use the Bailey Town Map to decide on an answer.
Write your answers on the lines below.

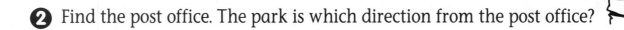

1 Look at the legend. What symbol is used for a school?

_____

2 Find the post office. The park is which direction from the post office?

_____

3 Find Hill Road. Which directions does this street run?

_____

4 Find Lake Reed. Which direction is the school from here?

_____

5 Find the shopping center. Go northwest on Holly Drive until the map ends.
What three things would you pass?

_____

6 Find Hill Road. Which street would you take to get to the park?

_____

7 If you lived in a house at the south end of the map, which directions would
you drive to get to school?

_____

8 Find Lake Reed. What business is directly west of it?

_____

9 What three streets would you take to drive from the shopping center to the school?

_____

10 Find Park Street. Follow it North. What street does Park Street merge on to?

_____

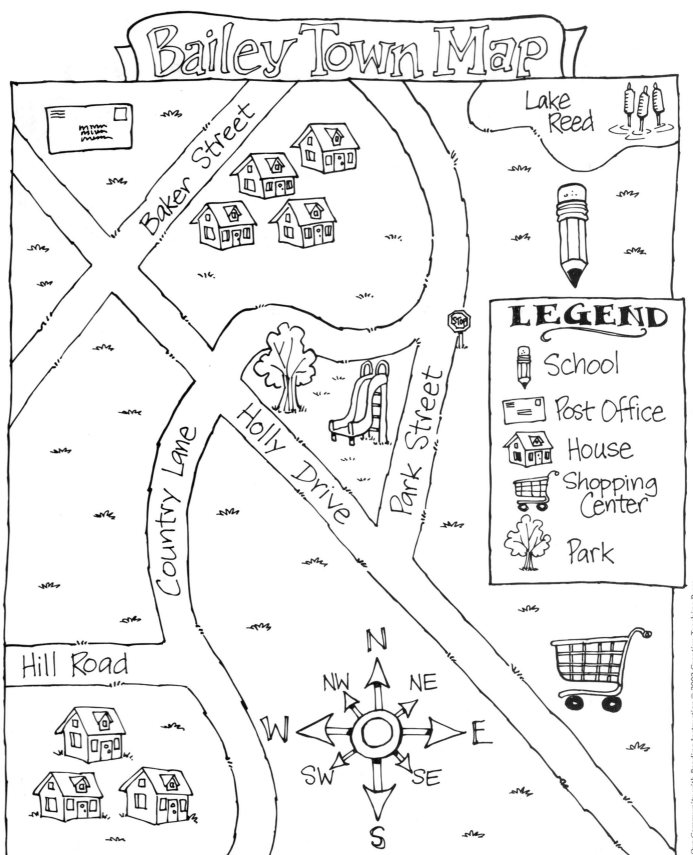

Integrating Our Community with Reading Instruction © 2002 Creative Teaching Press